HOW TO
DRIVE LIKE A MANIAC

THE *Self-Hurt* SERIES

KNOCK
KNOCK.
VENICE, CALIFORNIA

Published by
Knock Knock
1633 Electric Avenue
Venice, CA 90291
www.knockknock.biz

Illustrated by Mark Weber

ISBN: 978-160106041-9
UPC: 8-25703-50103-2

CHAPTER 6 .... **105**
Freeway Driving:
Faster, Faster, Faster!

CHAPTER 7 .... **125**
Neighborhood Driving:
Pedestrians, Etc.

CHAPTER 8 .... **151**
Multi-Tasking:
Your Right as a Maniac

CHAPTER 9 .... **167**
Parking:
It's Your Spot

CHAPTER 10 .... **189**
Conclusion:
A Maniac Among Maniacs

CONTENTS

CHAPTER 1 7
Introduction:
You Are the Center of the Universe

CHAPTER 2 23
They're All Idiots:
Getting into the Maniac Mindset

CHAPTER 3 47
Choose Your Weapon:
The Maniac Vehicle

CHAPTER 4 67
Rules of the Road:
They Don't Apply to You

CHAPTER 5 87
Communication:
Horns, Lights, Hand Gestures

YOU ARE THE CENTER OF THE UNIverse. On the roadway, unfortunately, you're constantly bombarded by idiots. Idiots who slow down so you can't run a red light. Idiots who put their feet on the brakes at the slightest drop of rain. Idiots who snatch that parking spot you had your eye on. All in all, they're in your way.

But you aren't going to put up with this any longer. Even if you're the kind of person who uses your turn signal or lets one of the idiots merge in front of you, this book will pump up your driving mojo. It's time to return the road to its rightful owner—you. It's time to drive like a maniac.

These days Americans spend more time in their cars than ever before—an average of an hour and a half per day. Do you want to be stuck in the car for so long *and* stuck behind some chump? If you're a pushover on the road when you have tons of metal surrounding you, how can you expect to stand up to your boss, your coworkers, your friends, or your significant other? You're number one, and you're going to take that attitude to the road. You owe it to your friends, your family, your health, your country, and, most importantly, yourself, to become a maniac driver.

With the tips and tricks contained in this book, you'll take control of the road and come to accept that driving like a maniac is your God-given right. You will no longer need to tolerate idiot drivers—for the first time, you'll actually be able to do

Join the Crowd!

- More than 64 percent of people are driving less courteously and more dangerously than they were 5 years ago.

- 80 percent of drivers are angry most or all of the time while driving.

something about them. Aren't you tired of driving safely and with consideration of others? Aren't you sick of wasting your time with stop signs and traffic laws? Don't despair, because you've taken the first step by reading this book. You're going to learn how to:

- Choose the perfect maniac vehicle and customize it for maximum intimidation, vision blockage, and gas guzzling.

- Get there faster.

- Ignore rules of the road.

- Perfect techniques like swerving and shoulder-driving.

- Turn left from the right lane and right from the left lane.

- Stop stopping for pedestrians.

- Get over your conscience and consideration of others.

There are so many benefits to driving like a maniac, some you may never have realized. Curious? Read on. As the center of the universe, you have no time to waste.

Saving Your Precious Time

Following the generally accepted rules of the road takes time—wasted time. Stop. Signal. Wait. Go Slowly. You've got better things to do. This is your life. And you're going to squander it just because of some silly speed limit when nobody's paying attention? Not anymore.

By driving like a maniac, you'll shave seconds and even minutes off of every trip you take. You'll zip through construction zones that would otherwise lengthen your commute. You'll zoom through neighborhoods and make pedestrians wish they'd never ventured into the crosswalk. You'll save seconds that you would never otherwise get back.

Even safety advocates and government bureaucrats acknowledge that spending more time in automobiles is bad for you. But because they also want you to drive slowly and obey traffic laws, however, their alternatives come with their own downsides:

- Leave earlier or later (*and waste more time*).

- Live closer to work (*by selling your house and moving to a neighborhood you don't like*).

- Alter your work schedule (*and lose your job*).

- Work at home (*and pay for your own coffee*).

The officials would have you change your life just to avoid traffic, but there's a better way to save time. Once you value your life above everyone else's, driving like a maniac is the only answer.

Saving Your Precious Skin

Driving like a maniac could also save your life. Authorities like the Department of Motor Vehicles, the federal government, and your driver's-ed teacher say that slower driving is safer for you, but the truth is that driving faster and more aggressively will save your neck.

The number-one federal government authority on automobile safety, the National

Highway Traffic Safety Administration, claims that speeding is "one of the most prevalent factors contributing to traffic crashes." But their own figures suggest that only 30 percent of cars involved in fatal crashes in 2005 were speeding. Speeding is therefore the safer way to drive 70 percent

Virtual Maniacs

Improve your maniac driving style even when you're not behind the wheel—with video games! A 2007 study conducted for the American Psychological Association proved that playing violent driving or car-racing games directly increased maniac behavior on the road. Here are some tips to choosing games and how to play them:

- Go for cover illustrations of souped-up cars, maniacal drivers, and frightened-looking pedestrians.

- Look for the "adult content" sticker.

- While you're playing, picture yourself transferring those moves to your real-world driving.

- Set goals—start at the lowest level and work your way up!

of the time. The reason? It's easier to get away from the idiots causing all the accidents if you're going faster.

The maniac knows there are so many more benefits to going faster versus idling behind some chump:

- Drivers who spend a significant amount of time behind the wheel face a greater risk of developing skin cancer, according to a recent study by St. Louis University School of Medicine. The next time you pass someone on the shoulder and they flip you off, shout back that you're simply trying to avoid getting melanoma.

- Each hour spent in a car causes a 6 percent increase in the likelihood of obesity, as recently calculated in a paper published in the *American Journal of Preventative*

Medicine. When a police officer pulls you over for doing 62 in a school zone, tell him you don't want to be another statistic in America's obesity epidemic.

- Spending more time in traffic harms the economy by decreasing worker productivity and making American companies less competitive in the global marketplace. The Texas Transportation Institute estimates that in 2003, congestion in this country caused 3.7 billion hours of delay, costing Americans $63 billion. If someone honks their horn at you because you cut them off, tell them it's for the sake of the trade deficit.

- Wasting time on the road wastes gasoline, which you need for your high-powered Hummer (see chapter 3). It's your right as an American to own the

Men vs. Women: Maniac Gender Splits

Men report doing each of these maniac driving behaviors more than women, but not by much! We're well on our way to maniac equality.

Maniac Behavior	Men	Women
Making an illegal turn	18%	12%
Not signaling lane changes	26%	20%
Following very closely	15%	13%
Going through red lights	9%	7%
Swearing, name-calling	59%	57%
Speeding 15 to 25 MPH	46%	32%
Yelling at another driver	34%	31%
Honking to protest	39%	36%
Revving engine to retaliate	12%	8%
Making an insulting gesture	28%	20%
Tailgating dangerously	14%	9%
Shining brights to retaliate	25%	13%
Braking suddenly to punish	35%	29%
Deliberately cutting off	19%	10%
Using car to block the way	21%	13%
Using car as weapon to attack	4%	1%
Chasing a car in hot pursuit	15%	4%
Getting into a physical fight	4%	1%

From "Dealing with Pressure and Stress in the Vehicle," by Leon James and Diane Nahl, in *Driving Lessons: Exploring Systems that Make Traffic Safer*, ed. J. Peter Rothe (Edmonton: University of Alberta Press, 2002).

biggest, loudest, most powerful car you want, and if some compact-owning individual is using up all the gas by sitting in traffic, that's less for your industrial-strength vehicle. The next time you floor it through a red light, honk your own horn and yodel, "God Bless America!"

As you can see, driving like a maniac is good for you. And while you probably don't care that it might be good for society, you do at least have greater justification for your actions when confronted by others who care about that sort of thing, like police officers, traffic court judges, or your mother.

Once you've justified your maniac driving proudly and boldly for the first time, you'll experience a surge in your personal power!

Feel More Powerful

Being number one should come naturally to you. If not, driving like a maniac will help. For better or worse, survival of the fittest is the law of nature, and self-interest is the law of the marketplace. Being number one should be your law of the roadway. And being number one behind the wheel will benefit your attitude in the rest of your life.

The percentage of Americans who enjoy driving has reached an all-time low, and it's probably no coincidence that many Americans also suffer from self-esteem problems, holding them back in all areas of their lives. If you're not a dominant human being while protected by your SUV, Mercedes, or blacked-out, oversized Hummer, how can you possibly dominate friends, coworkers, enemies, and in-laws?

Driving like a maniac is guaranteed to pump up your ego by making the roadway your own personal playground. Remember, it's your right as an American. Many Americans spend more time commuting to work than on vacation. So you deserve to enjoy your time on the road! Not only will this book will show you how to bring pleasure back into your driving, it will be the beginning of your complete transformation into a new, healthier, more lead-footed you.

Master of the Road

Even if you don't know it already, you are the center of the universe, and with the help of this book, you will be the center of the driving universe. You've just seen the many benefits of driving like a maniac—not only for the road, but for your entire life. But there's so much more to learn.

Like any worthwhile life change, driving like a maniac starts in the head. Next you'll learn how to change your attitude and adopt the maniac mindset.

CHAPTER 2
THEY'RE ALL IDIOTS: GETTING INTO THE MANIAC MINDSET

MOST AMERICANS ARE CONFORMISTS, content to follow the flow of traffic, so to speak—and they become idiot drivers who slow down at intersections, use their turn signals, and let pedestrians have the right-of-way. Not only is this behavior unnecessary, it's anathema to the maniac mindset. Even if you're one of these idiots, don't worry—this chapter will get you thinking like a maniac and overcoming your conscience in no time.

There are so many pressures to drive with consideration of others—laws, the media, traffic cops, other drivers, passengers, grisly accidents. But you can learn to ignore all

Fewer Roads, More Idiots

While the number of miles driven has increased by 35 percent since 1987, only 1 percent more roads have been built. It gets worse: between 1980 and 1999, the miles of vehicle travel increased by 76 percent, while the total miles of highways increased by only 1.5 percent, according to the Transportation Development Foundation. If roads aren't being built fast enough to carry all the people who now drive on them, what's the result? Traffic and congestion, the maniac's biggest enemy. Since they won't build the roads for you, you've got no choice but to take matters in your own hands.

that. In this chapter, we'll knock down the mental obstacles one by one, like construction pylons, and before long you'll be driving 95 miles per hour and playing chicken with weaker-willed drivers on the freeway. If you think like a maniac, you'll drive like a maniac. Here are some of the concepts we'll review:

- Channeling the racecar-driver mentality and absorbing the competitive spirit.

- Using your anger at the idiots to overcome any doubts about driving like a maniac.

- Teaching the idiot drivers a lesson when they make idiot moves.

- Conquering foolish, defeatist attitudes like "What about the laws?" and "What about the cops?"

While this transformation may seem daunting or stressful, it's by no means impossible—indeed, with the help of this book and your admirable desire to drive like a maniac, it's completely achievable. Keep in mind that if everybody could drive like a maniac, they would. With your commitment to becoming a maniac, you're already way ahead of the idiots. And the more red lights you run, the easier it gets.

Adopting the Maniac Attitude

When you look through your windshield at the maniacs and their fingers flying by you, it's all too easy to conclude that they were born maniacs. What you don't see is the years of effort and hard work behind their commendable behavior. Remember that you've got many years of idiot thinking to overcome. Your attitude just needs a tune-up and some practice to get in the right frame of mind.

Unlearn What You've Learned

Perhaps your parents were good drivers. Or maybe you got an *A* in driver's-ed and you can hear your instructor's voice telling you to drive defensively. Just like other aspects of your youthful education, in adulthood you realize that the teachers weren't always right. Driving defensively is one such falsehood. Not only does it waste your time, it doesn't protect you from the defensively driving idiots. If everybody's driving defensively, where's the offense? How will anything ever move at a four-way stop? Without an offensive game, there's no scoring, and nobody wins. Driving defensively goes against human nature. Think back to the selfishness that led you to triumph over all the other sperm when you were being conceived. The maniac attitude is the most primal and natural of all instincts—not the timid, defensive driving you've been taught.

Own the Road

Instead of believing you're sharing the road with others, think about how all those people are driving on *your* road. *Your* car. *Your* lane. *Your* turn. *You, you, you.* Don't let anyone tell you differently. Perhaps you've heard a self-righteous idiot say something like, "I didn't see your name on that parking spot!" Your reply should be "Damn right, my name is on that spot. And if you can't see it, you must be blind!" This is America, and there's enough to go around. Let them drive somewhere else if they're not happy. It's *your* road.

Channeling Mario Andretti

One of the best ways to absorb the maniac mentality is to start viewing yourself as a racecar driver. Every-body has a racecar driver within. Maybe you remember the first time

> ## Maniac Lingo: The Nanny Car
>
> A nanny car is a vehicle, generally a minivan or soccer-mom SUV, with built-in technologies to "help" drivers by thinking for them: buzzers that beep when you get too close to something ahead or behind; systems to park your car for you; blaring alerts when someone is in your blind spot; and even breathalyzers attached to ignition controls. It's bad enough that the seat belt reminder beeps incessantly—avoid the purchase or installation of these systems at all costs!

you sped downhill in a bicycle. Perhaps you liked to beat your little sister in go-kart races. Did you ever drag-race in high school? It's all about finding that competitive spirit on the adult roadway.

Try a few tricks to ease your way in, like watching auto racing on television or getting a NASCAR sticker for your back window. Take up a competitive sport and play with a "winning is everything" attitude. Whatever the discipline, you want to find a way to feel good about competing against others and winning, then move that mindset to the roadway.

Getting Angry

Feeling a sense of anger toward other drivers is critical to achieving the maniac mindset. The anger will help you overcome the pressures to drive like the idiots. If you're angry enough, you won't even have to think about what you're doing—you'll just hit the gas.

The beauty of anger is that it can be displaced, redirected from one cause to another. If you're having trouble mustering fury at other drivers, start thinking about the government morons who haven't done enough to solve traffic problems. Listen to the news—you can always find something to rage about in current events. Mull over everything in the world and in your life that bothers you, and think about everybody who's ever done you wrong. Try getting into the car pre-angry, perhaps by picking a fight with a coworker or your spouse. Once you're good and hot, take it out on fellow drivers.

Teach Them a Lesson

Not only are you better than everybody else, now you've got superior knowledge about how to drive. You can use your vast understanding to help develop a holier-than-thou attitude

on the roadway. When you're on the
street, consider yourself the teacher
and everyone else the students. If the
idiots do something stupid, it's your
duty to respond, whether by honking,
gesturing, squealing your tires, rev-

The Maniac Cinephile

Most authorities agree that maniac-worthy car
chases started in 1968 with *Bullitt*, starring the
ultimate maniac, Steve McQueen. Watch these
movies to get some pointers:

Bullitt (1968)

The French Connection (1971)

Gone in 60 Seconds (1974)

Smokey and the Bandit (1977)

The Blues Brothers (1980)

Speed (1994)

The Rock (1996)

Ronin (1998)

Transporter (2002)

Bourne Identity (2002)

ving your engine, or tailgating (see chapter 5). If you don't let them know the error of their ways, they're likely to make the same mistakes over and over again. You're the master—let them learn from you.

Overcoming Common Excuses and Obstacles

Transforming yourself into a maniac is a challenging process, and you may still have some lingering questions or fears. We'll dismantle those one by one, but overall, it's important to remember that excuses and obstacles are for idiots. Over time, as a maniac driver, you'll learn how to vanquish these annoyances.

"What about the laws?"

There are many traffic laws designed to keep the idiots in line. However, they don't apply to maniacs. Think of them merely as suggestions. Traffic laws actually give the maniac a useful edge; because others are observing the rules, you can predict what they're likely to do. For idiots, traffic laws should be considered ironclad edicts, and you're going to hold the idiots to them. In fact, at times you're going to go crazy when others violate the law.

It may take some time to develop this lawless attitude. But when you do, it will feed your sense of entitlement and yield an increased sense of freedom. Whenever you feel tempted to obey a law, try repeating to yourself, "This is my road. I can do whatever I want."

"What about the cops?"

While traffic laws should mean little to the maniac, there are, unfortunately, people hired to enforce them. But police officers didn't sign up for the academy to write tickets. They enlisted so *they* could drive fast and violate traffic laws. Pay attention to the way cops drive— they are some of the maniac's best role models. How many times have you seen police officers speeding for no apparent reason, or whizzing through busy traffic on the shoulder? They park wherever they choose, and they seem to think turn signals are a sign of weakness.

Nonetheless, it's not like there's some maniac ID you can flash to get yourself out of a ticket should you get pulled over, so you'll want to get a radar detector (see chapter 3). If you do get an officer on your tail, remember that cops love a good chase. These will be the moments when all your maniac training comes into play. And there are now so many laws restricting the way that the police handle high-speed pursuits, chances are that if you drive aggressively enough, they'll have to give up and let you go.

Maniac Populations

Maniacs can either choose to live among their own kind, or somewhere where they can take advantage of the idiots!

Cities with the Most Maniacs	Cities with the Fewest Maniacs
1. Miami	1. Portland
2. New York	2. Pittsburgh
3. Boston	3. Seattle–Tacoma
4. Los Angeles	4. St. Louis
5. Washington, DC	5. Dallas–Fort Worth

AutoVantage, "Road Rage Survey Reveals Best, Worst Cities," Affinion Group Media, May 15, 2007.

Not only will they secretly respect you for it, they'll have a great story to tell their buddies.

"What about the other drivers?"

Almost all drivers out there will tell you they're great drivers. By great, however, they mean slow and defensive. The idea that this constitutes greatness is far from the truth, and the accident statistics just don't back their assertions up. Not only have you observed this from personal experience, you know you're a better driver than those idiots. How you handle your attitude toward the other drivers, however, is one of the biggest determinants in your maniac success.

When you start to drive like a maniac, other drivers may appear upset with you. They will honk, scream, shout, or swerve. They may flip you off, say nasty things, or even post derogatory comments about you on the Internet. Despite the fact that you should be the one upset at them, the most important

Places to Avoid: Traffic Congestion

In 2003, according to the Texas Transportation Institute, the areas of the country with the highest traffic delay per traveler (equally applied to both idiots and maniacs) were:

1. Los Angeles–Long Beach–Santa Ana
2. San Francisco–Oakland
3. Washington, DC
4. Atlanta
5. Houston
6. Dallas–Fort Worth–Arlington
7. Chicago
8. Detroit
9. Riverside–San Bernardino
10. Orlando

thing to remember as a maniac is
that you don't care. Whatever they do,
you don't care. And of course you can
always "communicate" right back at
them (see chapter 5).

"What about society?"

Society imposes quite a bit of pressure
to drive with caution. These damaging
messages come from the media, government, and even your own friends
and family. While it's easy to say you
don't care about the rest of the world,
sometimes, despite yourself, you do. It's
helpful in these moments to remind
yourself that you don't care what they
have to say about anything else, so
why listen to them about driving?

Often a beginning maniac driver will
witness an accident, narrowly escape

one, or catch a glimpse of one on the evening news. This can be enough to send some individuals back to defensive driving. This doesn't have to be you, however. When you do see an accident, remember that it was most likely caused by a stupid, slow driver who lost life or limb while aggressive, maniac drivers zoomed past. In any case, don't focus on other people's tragedies—they're not you, and you need to think about yourself. Remember the maniac mantra: I am the center of the universe.

If you're having trouble banishing society's voices from your head, consider countering the barrage of public-safety messages with maniac messages. Keep racing magazines and photos nearby. Watch movies

The Ultimate Maniac-Mobile: The Hummer

AM General, builder of the "toughest trucks on the planet" and vehicle supplier to the United States military, first started rolling High Mobility Multi-Purpose Wheeled Vehicles (Humvees) off the assembly line in 1985. At the behest of the ultimate maniac, Arnold Schwarzenegger, the company started building civilian models in 1992. Upon receiving his vehicle, Schwarzenegger exclaimed, "Look at those deltoids! Look at those calves!" The Hummer is a gratifying reflection of the increasing militarization of our society, bringing militainment to the streets. Even McDonald's got into the game, helping to develop young maniacs with a 2006 Happy Meal that included a toy Hummer. The Hummer gets 10 miles per gallon in the city, but that's not its best feature. Because it's a class-3 truck, like shuttle buses and ambulances, it's exempt from EPA ratings and many safety rules, like seat belts. It can drive through water up to 30 inches deep, climb a 60 percent grade, and make mincemeat of a 22-inch vertical wall. Never mind if you don't actually *do* any of those things—the fact that it makes you look like a maniac is reason enough to spend almost $150,000 on an H1!

with high-speed car chases. When you perform a successful maniac driving maneuver, replay it over and over again in your mind.

Soon you'll chuckle at the chumps who drive "safely." You'll get a kick out of those cute little "Buckle Up" billboards. And most importantly, you'll stand as a powerful stalwart in the face of society's pressures.

"What about my conscience?"

Many pupils find that even after they've learned all the maniac techniques and overcome the objections of others, there is still a little voice saying that driving aggressively is wrong. If this happens to you, don't listen! Tell that voice very simply, "Thank you for sharing," and repeat to yourself, "I am the center of the universe." Soon your conscience will disappear completely.

Thinking the Maniac Way

You're well on your way to having the mindset of the maniac—doesn't it feel great? You may need to refer back to this chapter as you progress in your transformations. Sometimes you'll take three steps forward then two back—that's natural—but the most important thing is not to let any slippage impair your confidence. Keeping your head in the game is critical to becoming the best maniac you can be, so by all means reread this chapter whenever you need a boost. One helpful tool for maintaining this disciplined state of mind is having a constant reminder of who you are at your maniac best every time you step in the car. What better way than to have that reminder *be* your car? Read on to learn how to acquire and customize your own personal maniac vehicle.

CHAPTER 3
CHOOSE YOUR WEAPON: THE MANIAC VEHICLE

WHILE THE MANIAC MINDSET IS THE internal manifestation of the anti-idiot worldview, the vehicle is its exterior, visible expression. There can be no driver without a car, and thus there can be no maniac without the appropriately superior machine.

Of course it's best to start from scratch when becoming a maniac, selecting a new, powerful car to reflect your new values. However, becoming a maniac doesn't require wealth, and, with the help of a few accessories, the committed maniac can overcome the wimpiest of vehicles—even, heaven forbid, a Prius.

Your goal in choosing or equipping your car for maximum mania is intimidation, power, and speed. You don't want the idiot drivers to be able to see over, around, or through your vehicle, and you want them to eat your dust. You'll also want to equip your car with all the add-ons you need to rule the road. In this chapter, we'll review:

- The pros and cons of a sports car versus an SUV versus a pickup.

- How modifications such as tinted windows and extra headlights can increase your intimidation power.

- The mandatory radar detector.

Name that Car

A Colorado State University study discovered that people who name their cars or assign them a gender are more likely to be aggressive drivers.

What's Your Maniac Model?

When choosing a car, many maniac drivers face the dilemma of whether to purchase a sports car or an SUV. On the one hand, the sports car is nimble and fast, allowing you to outmaneuver and outspeed the idiots, not to mention pricking their envy. Alternatively, SUVs intimidate other drivers and block their vision while allowing you a clear, high view of the road. As a special bonus, SUV drivers are viewed as impatient, inconsiderate, and selfish—that's you!

But consider a third alternative: the large pickup truck. Many people are downright afraid of pickup drivers, especially if they have tinted windows and a gun rack. What's more, the facts support their fears. A 2005 study found that large pickup trucks pose the greatest risks to other drivers. Smaller pickups and SUVs were second on the list of harm-causing vehicles, but they trailed large pickups considerably. Sports cars actually posed a greater risk to their drivers than to others.

While sports cars can be tricked out to intimidate, both SUVs and pickups illustrate a maniac dynamic known as "the rule of tonnage": simply put, the bigger your vehicle the better. The bigger your vehicle, the more idiot drivers are apt to get out of your way. The bigger your vehicle, the more invincible you'll feel and the more risks you'll be willing to take.

Having a big vehicle means you're more imposing in the rearview mirror. Because a reckless and large vehicle has an impact on other drivers not unlike Moses parting the

Maniac Safety

According to a study that examined car models from 1997 to 2001, the top-ten most dangerous vehicles to other drivers were all pickups:

1. Dodge Ram 3500
2. Chevy/GMC C/K3500
3. Ford F-350
4. Dodge Ram 2500
5. Ford F-250
6. Chevy/GMC C/K2500
7. Dodge Ram 1500
8. Dodge Dakota
9. Ford F-150
10. Chevy/GMC C/K1500

From "The Effects of Vehicle Model and Driver Behavior on Risk," by Thomas P. Wenzel and Marc Ross, in *Accident Analysis and Prevention* 37 (2005).

Red Sea, it's easier to force your way into a tight line of cars. And you're more likely to survive the eventual idiot-caused accident.

When choosing your large car or truck, always get more car than you need. This applies doubly if you're small in stature or any other area—you'll want to compensate with a bigger, more powerful car. Just as it's not necessary to carry passengers or cargo in order to merit getting a big vehicle, neither should you ever go off-road to justify choosing four-wheel drive. Most SUV drivers never drive off-road, though the capability can come in handy when you have to use the shoulder.

After-Market Modifications

While picking the right vehicle is important, you can't stop there. After-market modifications are essential to the maniac driver. With the help of a good mechanic and body shop, not to mention a few easy accessories, you can make your vehicle bigger and scarier than you'd ever believe possible.

Body Lifts

Once you have a big vehicle, you can make it even bigger with a body lift or suspension lift. A body lift simply raises the car's body with spacers added to the frame mounts. A suspension lift, or lift kit, modifies the vehicle's springs, shocks, controlling arms, and steering linkage. The advantages to lifting are not to be overstated. You'll be able to see over all other vehicles, put on bigger, more intimidating tires, and, best of all, easily run over almost anything—including compact cars.

Tires

Big, thick tires with dramatic treads are the way to go, preferably set off by special hubcaps or rims. Besides boosting the all-important intimidation factor, bigger tires will support some maniac maneuvers too stressful for smaller, cheaper tires. Remember—you may need to take your vehicle places it wasn't intended to go.

Tinted Windows

Tinted windows are a must—and not just to evade the increasingly popular red-light cameras. You want the advantage of being able to see other drivers without their being able to see you. Being behind your own one-way glass will make it psychologically easier to treat other drivers with contempt. Whenever you want the idiots to see you flipping them off, you can always roll down the window.

Headlights

Give your mechanic a few extra bucks to have your headlights pointed higher than legally allowed. Whether through their rearview mirror or head-on, tilted-up headlights get people's attention. People almost always back down when they're being blinded, allowing you to go right past them. Extra headlights, mounted on your grille or your roof, have a similar effect.

Muffler

Noise announces your presence from around a corner or behind an alley, so get your factory muffler replaced by a noisy one. Once they hear that deep rumble, the idiots will start looking around, off-guard before they even see you coming. The risk of a fix-it ticket is worth it because you won't just blow by, you'll *roar* by. It goes without saying that if you're lucky enough to have a broken muffler already, don't fix it.

Horn

The horn is one of the maniac's most vital communication devices, and you're going to be using it a lot, hitting it hard and for long periods of time. The horn your car comes with may not be loud enough, but you can replace it with a considerably more resonant aftermarket version. Because idiot drivers can become desensitized to all the horns they hear on the road, you might even consider a musical horn to break through the cacophony. And you can entertain yourself and your friends for hours by playing "La Cucaracha" over and over again while your car is just sitting in the driveway.

License Plates

License plates are an unnecessary evil, and you may want to consider leaving them off entirely. Keep them in your trunk in case you get pulled over—you can always say you're on your way to purchase the mounting screws. Another option is to cover them with tinted plastic to save yourself from red-light cameras. The front license plate is optional in several states, and many maniacs enjoy replacing it with Confederate flag artwork.

Inside the Maniac-Mobile: Gear

For the dedicated maniac, what you have inside your car can be as important as the car itself. Once you've modified your vehicle, there are a number of accessories that you'll want to buy.

Radar Detector

Also known as a fuzzbuster, the radar detector is the only mandatory piece of equipment for the maniac driver. Because you are going to be traveling at high rates of speed,

Repeat After Me

To get into the appropriate maniac mindset, you might want to try some motivational listening, especially in the car:

- Interviews with racecar drivers.

- Soundtracks from high-adrenaline movies.

- Recordings of the audio track of car chases.

- Sounds of screeching tires and motors revving, from auto races or films.

- Your own voice, repeatedly stating "I am the center of the universe."

- Fast-moving, hard-driving, and/or anger-inducing music.

- Nature sounds such as grizzly bears growling, hyenas fighting, etc.

- Anything that pumps you up.

performing risky maneuvers, and generally ignoring traffic laws, it's a priority to avoid getting caught. Not only do you want to save money on fines and keep your license, only idiot drivers attend traffic school.

Car Stereo

Lacking in both volume and bass, factory-installed car stereos are never adequate for the maniac driver. As a maniac, you want to rattle bones, and for that, you need custom components. At the most basic level, you'll need a special stereo, an amplifier, additional speakers, and a subwoofer. Tell the specialist at the stereo shop that you want people to feel your stereo when they're in another car—several lanes away. You want to wake people up. Ideally, you want the sound of your car stereo to arrive home several minutes before you do.

Television Sets

While vehicular television sets are not necessary for the maniac driver, they provide entertainment and luxury during inevitable traffic slowdowns that cannot be escaped by maniac maneuvers. However, the beginning maniac should not install them early in the learning process, as anger in response to traffic is a key part of developing the maniac mindset (see chapter 2).

There are two types of television to have installed in the car. One plays for passengers in the backseat, a useful accessory to distract them from criticizing your irreproachable driving. The other plays in the dashboard, though in order to watch it while you drive, you must remove the disabling device that prevents the front-seat television from working while the vehicle is in motion. And thanks to your window tint, police officers won't be able to see that your television is operational.

The Maniac Palette: Color Choices

Contrary to popular belief, red and yellow cars do not receive the most speeding tickets—it's actually white and silver! Green cars get in the most accidents, probably because only idiots choose green. The best maniac choice is black. One urban legend tells of a black car with a muffled engine and no running lights zooming past police officers night after night because the cops couldn't see the vehicle. How did the driver manage it? Night-vision goggles.

Not only will the television prove an entertaining addition to your maniac-level multi-tasking skills (see chapter 8), you'll be able to keep up with breaking local news to avoid traffic snarls.

Seat Belts

Whether or not to wear a seat belt is an individual maniac decision. Some maniac drivers prefer to exercise their personal freedom by not wearing them, while others feel emboldened knowing they're strapped in and ready to conquer the road.

Other Essentials

At this point, your vehicle should be all but maniac-ready. However, in addition to your gear, there are two last items necessary for embarking on the road.

Insurance

Many aspiring maniac drivers will think, "Why do I need insurance? I'm never going to get in an accident." While you will be vastly more adept at getting away from the idiot drivers who cause all the accidents, in the unlikely event that you are involved, everything

Maniac Lingo: Cup-Holder Cuisine

A term coined by the food industry to reflect the design of new food products engineered to fit into cup-holders, like cereal, soup, and yogurt. Also known as *dashboard dining*.

will be paid for. Additionally, insurance will help embolden your behavior and eliminate any lingering guilt you may harbor. Ultimately insurance allows you to do whatever you want, and thus puts the "man" in maniac.

Sunglasses

Sunglasses are an essential maniac prop, even at night. First, they prevent eye contact between you and pedestrians or other drivers who may mistake eye contact for vulnerability. Second, should anything go wrong while you're driving, sunglasses will make you harder to identify in a lineup. Third, they will prevent red-light cameras from fully disclosing your identity, giving you plausible deniability. The best sunglasses for your purposes are dark or mirrored and preferably wraparound. As with the tinted windows, should you want to "communicate" with other drivers, you can always whip the sunglasses off and make meaningful eye contact.

Ready to Roll

This is a proud moment for you, the aspiring maniac driver. Not only are you adopting the maniac mentality, you have your vehicle—your external skin—outfitted for maximum performance and intimidation. What's next? It's time to hit the road and learn how the rules don't apply to you.

CHAPTER 4
RULES OF THE ROAD: THEY DON'T APPLY TO YOU

OTHER THAN "I AM THE CENTER OF the universe," there are no rules of the road for the maniac driver. Instead, the maniac drives with a general sense of lawlessness and disrespect for authority. The only rules are those that *you* decide upon. *Your* road. *Your* vehicle. *Your* rules. That said, there are some general principles that will prove invaluable to you as a maniac driver. We'll show you:

- What a red light means to a maniac driver.

- Why a maniac driver pays attention to "speed," not "speed limits."

- The maniac thrills of mountain roads.

- How to scare your passengers.

General Rules:
Road Signs, Right-of-Way, and Speed

On the road we all encounter many signs to indicate what we should be doing. The trick to driving like a maniac is realizing that these signs mean different things to different drivers. Your job now is to learn how to interpret road signs like a maniac.

Red-Light Cameras

Red-light cameras are supposed to make us safer, but they do exactly the opposite. Studies show that rear-end collisions are dramatically increased—as much as 140 percent—at these intersections. What are they good for? Revenue, as evidenced by the fact that many jurisdictions that use the cameras *decrease* the length of those intersections' yellow lights. Shorter yellow lights are more dangerous, but shorter yellow lights plus traffic cameras generate revenue.

Common Signs and Signals

Memorize these alternate definitions for some of the common road signs you encounter on the roadway (some are covered more extensively in chapter 7):

Stop sign: Watch for drivers coming from other directions while going through the intersection.

Speed limit: What other people are going.

Turn only: Go straight if you want.

Yellow light: Floor it.

Red light: Look both ways, then floor it.

No U-turn: Keep an eye out for cops before turning around.

Yield: Make the other drivers yield.

Curve ahead: Use both lanes so you don't have to slow down.

School zone: Heavy fines if you don't get away fast.

No passing zone: Pass on the shoulder.

Remember—if you're not caught, you didn't really break the law.

You Have the Right-of-Way—Always

The number-one maniac rule of the road is that you have the right-of-way; if you have a hard time remembering that, try recalling that you're the center of the universe, as the two concepts go hand in hand. Who legally has the right-of-way in any particular situation? Who knows? Figuring out when to defer to another car—whether you're turning, merging, or at a stop sign—is an exercise in confusion, so don't. Instead, always take the initiative to go first. Even if it's obvious that you don't have the right-of-way—for example, when there's a yield sign—you can usually take the right-of-way simply by refusing to give in.

The operating procedure for this rule is simple: just keep going. Nine times out of ten, the other motorist will give in because they're scared you're going to hit them. You're using right-of-way confusion against them. Grabbing the right-of-way by sheer force of will—even when you don't necessarily deserve it—is what driving like a maniac is all about. You deserve the right-of-way at all times because they're idiot drivers and you're better than they are.

Speed

It's intentional that the name of this section is "Speed," not "Speed Limits." Your default driving technique should be to drive your vehicle as fast as you possibly can in any circumstance. Just focus on the "Speed" and not the "Limit." The numbers on the signs are just suggestions, the speed that idiots should drive, but not you. Here are a few reasons why:

- Speed limits, like most road rules, are designed to deter the really bad drivers, so they don't apply to you.

- Following the speed limits isn't really any safer.

- You have a radar detector.

- Most people are smart enough or fast enough to get out of the way in time.

Because speed is your most useful tool as a maniac driver, becoming comfortable with going considerably

---

Save the Autobahn!

On any given day, over half of the 7,500-mile-long autobahn in Germany has no speed limit, making those stretches the fastest public highways in the world. In 2007, the European Union's environment commissioner (not a German) called for environmentally friendly speed limits to be instituted on the entire autobahn. This notion was met with public outrage and massive resistance from politicians, automotive groups, and even the German chancellor and environment minister. Critics of the limits have pointed out that instituting a speed limit of 75 MPH would reduce Germany's auto emissions by less than 0.5 percent. Speeds on the autobahn average 93 MPH, but speeds reaching 185 MPH—the speed of a commercial jet upon takeoff—and higher do occur. The real kicker? The autobahn is statistically safer than most other highways.

faster than anyone else on the road is a significant step in your transformation. Once speeding becomes second nature to you, you'll learn to make a point of driving fast even when common sense would dictate a slower pace—for example, in school zones or around a funeral procession. We'll revisit speed in chapter 7.

Special Circumstances

Every once in a while, you'll come across unique driving circumstances that present golden opportunities for you to shine as a maniac driver. While they're rare enough that it can be difficult to remember what to do, fortunately the situational responses are natural for the maniac driver and your instincts will kick in.

Bad Weather

Bad weather is entirely overestimated as a road hazard. In some places, laws stipulate that you should drive slower than the posted speed limit if the weather is bad. But the maniac doesn't drive the posted speed limit on a clear day, so you certainly won't let a little rain, sleet, or snow slow you down.

Unfortunately, inclement weather usually slows the idiot drivers, presenting the maniac with obstacles to maneuver around. You'll want to move away from them quickly because they will start slipping and sliding. Bad weather also presents a great time to teach them a lesson (see chapter 2). If you can't get by, you may need to resort to honking or other aggressive communication

Drafting: Free Rides

Drafting is an ingenious technique you can use when emergency vehicles scream by. As soon as they pass, floor it and immediately get behind the last ambulance or police car, nose to tail if possible. The lead car cuts the wind resistance for you in front, and by being directly behind the leading vehicle, you cut the resistance from its rear, enabling both of you to go faster than you would separately. Also try this with semi-trucks on the highway. It doesn't matter whether you understand the physics involved—just know that it works!

(see chapter 5). Slowing down in bad weather is unnecessary if you know what you're doing.

Running Late

Whether or not you choose to arrive on time is up to you, but *never* leave on time. When you need to go somewhere, think first about when you want to arrive, and second about how long it will likely take you to get there. Then, leave much later. For example, if you need to be somewhere by 8:30 PM, and it takes 30 minutes to get there, leave at 8:15 PM This will ensure that you are rushed, which will amplify your aggressiveness. A hurried driver is a maniac driver.

Construction

Construction is a headache because it causes slowdowns. When you see the orange evidence of a construction zone, it's time to kick your driving up a notch. You do not, however, need to follow what those orange signs actually say. At the first indication of a construction zone, idiot drivers will slow down or begin merging away from a closed lane. You'll want to do the opposite. Speed up, and merge only at the very last second in front of the idiots who queued up far too early. If you need to, use the closed lane, or drive through the construction cones.

Curves

Roadway curves are romanticized in our culture. They indicate a time to slow down, veer off the path, enjoy the view. For the maniac, however, curves are an invitation to practice Formula One driving skills. To go as fast as possible, racecar drivers go straight through the curve, riding the inside then accelerating out of the curve's apex. On two-lane roads, this will entail using both lanes and perhaps pushing another driver onto the shoulder.

Passing

To pass or not to pass? Pass, whenever you want. The experienced
maniac driver also knows there are
ways to *create* passing opportunities
that don't exist for others. Don't be
afraid to use the shoulder if necessary. Flash your brights, use your
horn, or both to indicate that you
need to move ahead. Scare oncom-
ing vehicles off the road in order to
get by. And of course, don't ever let
anyone pass you.

Emergency Vehicles

Most people curse the sound of sirens
when they're navigating busy traffic.
However, as a maniac, you can use
emergency vehicles to your advantage.
As soon as the ambulance, police car,

or fire truck comes screaming behind you, you'll see every other car on the road pull to the side. Pretend as if you're doing the same, then get behind the emergency vehicle and let it part the busy traffic for you, an invaluable technique during rush hour. The emergency vehicles essentially provide you with your own personal motorcade escort, giving new meaning to the term "ambulance chaser."

Mountain Roads

Mountain roads offer more danger and excitement than almost any other driving environment. With steep inclines, winding curves, jaw-dropping cliffs, speed-gathering downhills, and emergency turnouts for out-of-control trucks, it's a veritable playground for

Maniac Lingo: The Lexus Lane

HOV (high-occupancy vehicle) lanes might one day become available to drivers who pay for the privilege of using the less congested lanes, dubbed *Lexus lanes*. A maniac would just use the lanes without paying for the privilege, of course!

the maniac driver. All your aggressive moves—attacking curves, swerving, speeding, tailgating (see chapters 6 and 7)—are magnified when you're facing the perils of a mountain road. Enjoy it while you can, and use all your tricks to your advantage.

Scaring Your Passengers

While it's the maniac's preference not to drive with nagging passengers, sometimes it's necessary to do so. In these instances, use your passengers as a maniac gauge. The more they complain or shudder, the more maniac skills you should implement. Use their objections to spur you on. If you respond to every objection with an increasingly aggressive driving maneuver, they'll be quiet soon enough.

Accidents

Accidents are bound to happen, but not necessarily to you. The potential for an accident should never influence your maniac driving. Instead, let the fear of accidents influence the *idiots'* driving. They can be the ones to hit the brakes, veer off the road, or slow down to avoid an accident. Don't waver, because your persistence is what will save you from an accident. Others may curse, "You could have caused an accident," but if you drove away intact, then you were successful.

If you do happen to find yourself in that split second before impact, speed up. You want to be the one with momentum. It's basic physics: an object in motion tends to stay in motion.

$$\textbf{Mass} \times \textbf{Velocity} = \textbf{Force}$$

Because the idiot you're going to hit will probably be braking, you'll do damage to them, not the other way around.

Practice Makes the Maniac

Now that you've learned your special rules of the road and how to take advantage of the thrilling driving challenges that may come your way, you'll want to practice as much as possible to polish your skills. Once you're secure in your understanding of the maniac rulebook, it will be time—believe it or not—to start communicating with the idiots.